SCIENCE
in Action
HOW THINGS WORK

LIGHT and DARK

Anna Claybourne

Quarto is the authority on a wide range of topics.

Quarto educates, entertains and enriches the lives of our readers—enthusiasts and lovers of hands-on living.

www.quartoknows.com

© 2016 Quarto Publishing plc

This paperback edition published in 2018
by QED Publishing,
an imprint of The Quarto Group.
The Old Brewery, 6 Blundell Street,
London N7 9BH, United Kingdom.
T (0)20 7700 6700 F (0)20 7700 8066
www.QuartoKnows.com

A catalogue record for this book is available from the British Library.

ISBN 978 1 78493 101 8

Manufactured in Guangdong, China TT032018

9 8 7 6 5 4 3 2 1

Publisher: Maxime Boucknooghe
Editorial Director: Victoria Garrard
Art Director: Miranda Snow
Series Editor: Claudia Martin
Series Designer: Bruce Marshall
Photographer: Michael Wicks
Illustrator: John Haslam
Consultant: Penny Johnson

Picture credits

t = top, b = bottom, c = centre, l = left, r = right,
fc = front cover

Getty Images 10–11 and 18l Dorling Kindersley
Shutterstock fc Gelpi JM, 4l Champiofoto,
4r Henrik Larsson, 5t 26kot, 5c, 7t Ianych, 7br kzww,
8 George Burba, 8–9 Kevin Key, 9r 3Dsculptor, 13l Paul
Matthew Photography, 15t Studio 1One, 15b Jan van der
Hoeven, 17 Michael D Brown, 19br Neil Wigmore,
20l Galushko Sergey, 20r fluidworkshop, 21l MilanB,
21r Graham R Prentice

MIX
Paper from responsible sources
FSC® C016973

Words in **bold** can be found in the glossary on page 22.

CONTENTS

Where is light from?

Most of our light comes from the Sun as **daylight**. The Sun is a star and it gives out lots of light and heat.

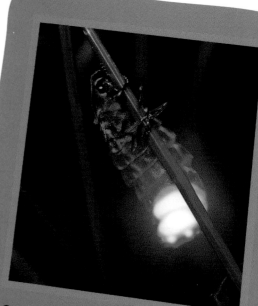

Another **light source** are electric lights. They use **electricity** to make light.

Some animals, such as this glow worm, glow with light! The light is caused by chemicals found in their body.

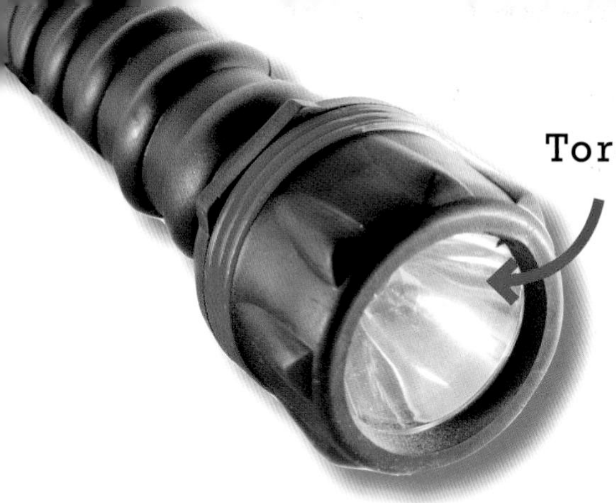

Torch

◀ Another source of light is a torch. It has a small light bulb that is powered by a battery.

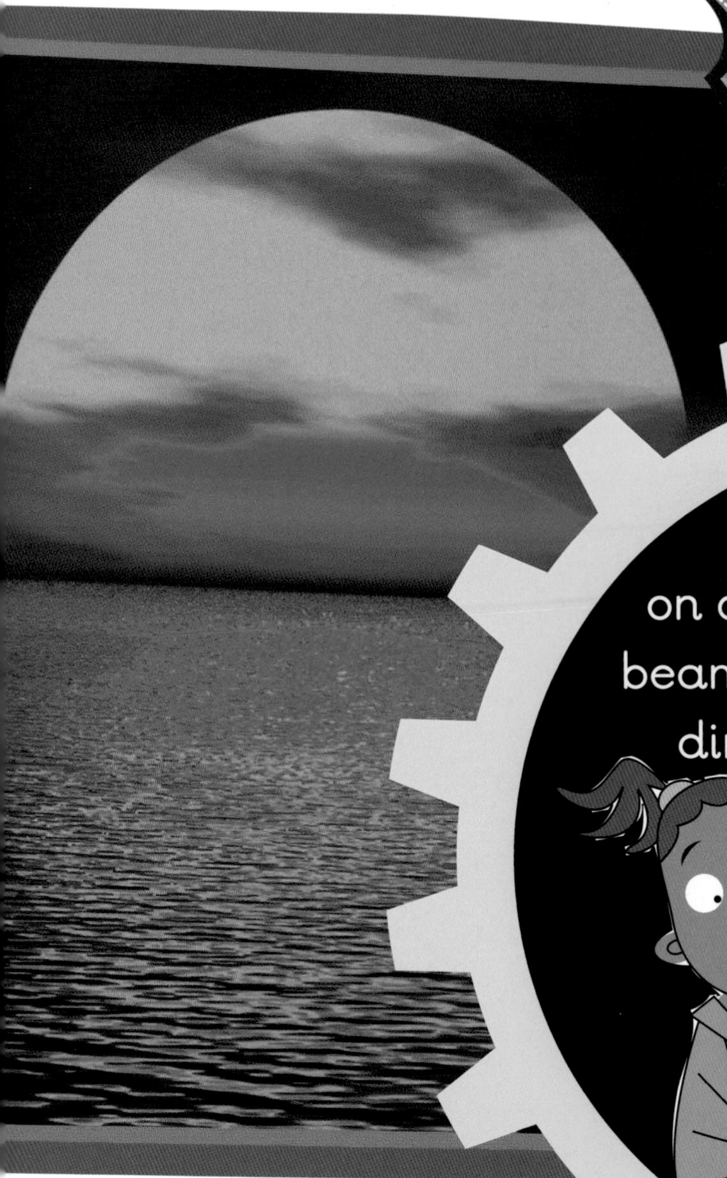

When you switch on a torch in the dark, a beam of light shines in the direction you point it.

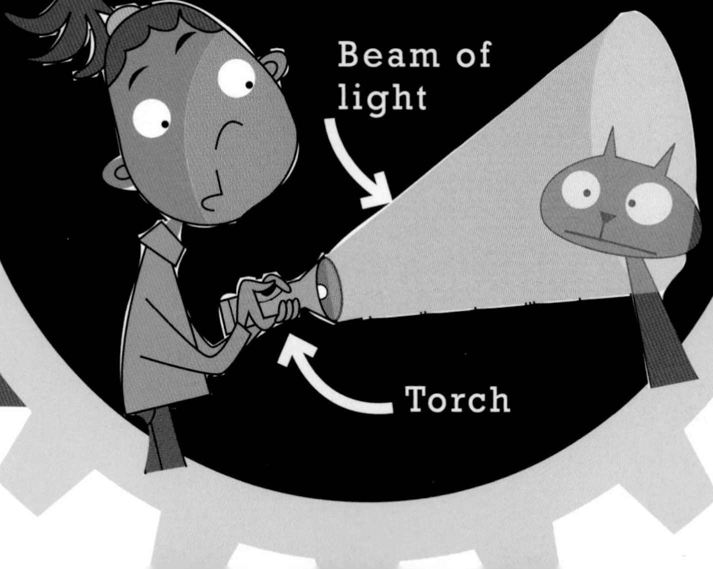

Beam of light

Torch

5

Light and sight

When you cover your eyes, you can no longer see. Why not? How does light help us to see?

Light has to go into your eyes for you to be able to see. If you close your eyes, or cover them with your hands, light no longer reaches them.

Your hands block light from reaching your eyes.

Light bulb

When you move your hands away, light reaches your eyes.

Rays of light

Light bounces off an object and into your eyes. That is how you can see it!

Light shines onto an object

Light bounces off an object

Light from the Sun or a light bulb shines straight into your eyes. Light also bounces off all the objects around you, before entering your eyes.

When light enters your eyes, a message is sent to your brain so you understand what you are looking at.

Pupil

Light goes into your eyes through holes called **pupils.**

How far can you see?

How far do you think your eyes can see. One kilometre? Ten kilometres? One thousand kilometres?

You can see much further than that! At night, you can see the Moon. It is about 400,000 kilometres away from the Earth.

From the top of a hill or tall building, you can see a very long way. As long as nothing blocks your view.

You can also see the stars at night. They are billions of kilometres away. Like the Sun, each star is a ball of fire. You can see the stars because light from them travels to your eyes.

Light moves incredibly fast. It travels about 300,000 kilometres every second!

Light moves much faster than speedy space rockets.

Shadows

Try shining a torch at a wall but putting your hands in the way. What happens?

The places light cannot reach remain dark.

Your hands block light from the torch. Materials that light cannot pass through are called **opaque**. Opaque objects cause **shadows**.

Light casts shadows because it travels in straight lines. It cannot curve around things.

A shadow is made when an object stops light getting through.

Shadow

Beam of light

Torch

It's a fact!

As the rays of light shine out of the torch, they spread out in straight lines. This makes the spider's shadow on the wall bigger than the spider itself.

Bouncing light

Light travels in straight lines. To go round a corner, it needs something to bounce off.

Light bounces off things all the time. For example, it can bounce, or **reflect**, off a mirror.

TRY THIS

Try using a small mirror to see round a corner.

1 Stand outside a room, next to the doorway, so that you cannot see inside.

2 Hold up the mirror so that it faces the room. Turn it slowly towards you. You will be able to see things inside the room reflected in the mirror.

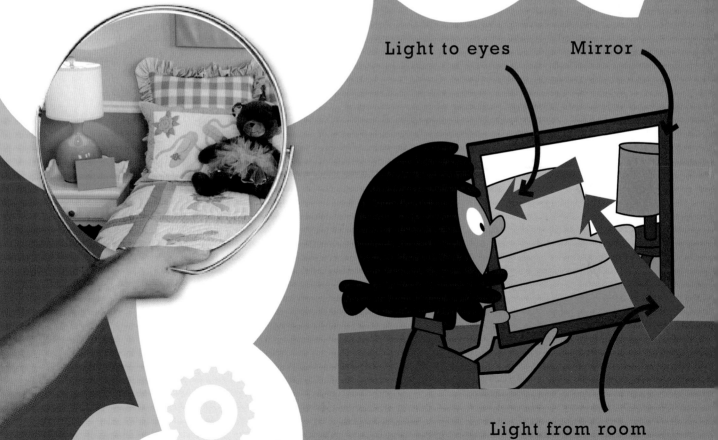

Light to eyes   Mirror

Light from room

Bending light

Light bends when it passes in and out of see-through substances, such as water and plastic. This is called refraction.

TRY THIS

Refraction can make a coin appear to move! You will need a coin, a clear bowl, some water and an adult to help you.

1 Place the coin at the bottom of the bowl. Sit facing the bowl so that you can see it from one side.

2 Keep very still and ask the adult to slowly fill the bowl with water. The coin seems to rise, although it is still sitting on the bottom.

Bowl   Coin

When you stand in a swimming pool, refraction makes your legs look shorter.

Light bends as it passes from water to air. It makes the coin look as though it has moved.

If you stand a pencil in a glass of water, refraction makes it look broken.

Water

Night on Earth

Our planet, Earth, is spinning. As it spins, the area we live in slowly faces towards the Sun, then turns away again. That's why it gets dark at night.

TRY THIS

You can see how this works using a torch, a ball on a string and a sticker.

1 Mark the place where you live by placing a sticker on the ball.

2 Make the room dark and shine the torch at the ball. Now spin the ball around on its string.

3 As the ball spins, the sticker moves into the light, then the dark just as the Earth does.

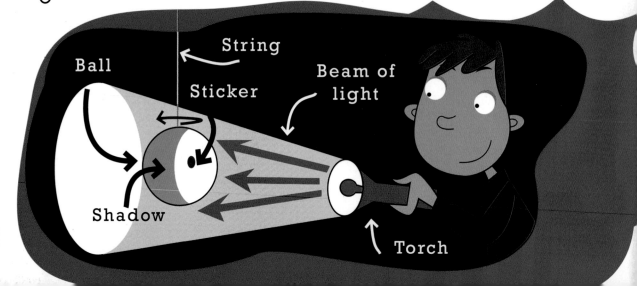

Ball · String · Sticker · Beam of light · Shadow · Torch

Day

Night

It's a fact!

Light cannot curve around the Earth. So the part facing away from the Sun is in shadow. The Sun never switches off so it's always daytime somewhere in the world.

When we're in the Sun's light, it's daytime. When we face away from the Sun, it's night.

Shadow clock

The Sun seems to move across the sky during the day but it is actually the Earth that moves. This means shadows also move.

TRY THIS

You can use shadows to tell the time. To make a shadow clock you will need a pencil, a straw, modelling clay, a paper plate and a clock or watch.

1 The straw needs to stand up in the middle of the plate. Use modelling clay to fix it to the plate.

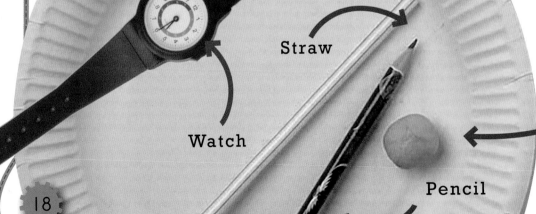

Paper plate

Watch

Straw

Modelling clay

Pencil

2 Put the plate in a sunny place where the Sun shines for most of the day. A windowsill is ideal.

3 Every hour, mark where the straw's shadow falls, then label it with the time.

Paper plate

Straw

3pm

Modelling clay

2pm

1pm

12pm

4 Keep the shadow clock in the same position. Now you can use it to tell the time. For example, whenever the shadow falls on the mark for 3 o'clock, it is 3 o'clock!

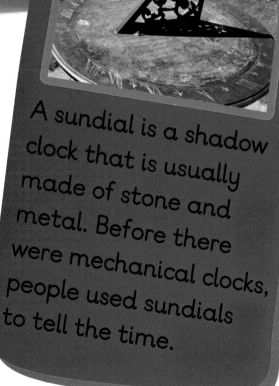

A sundial is a shadow clock that is usually made of stone and metal. Before there were mechanical clocks, people used sundials to tell the time.

The colours of light

Light from lamps and from the Sun looks white but it is actually made of many colours mixed together.

TRY THIS

The colours in light are revealed if you shine light through a triangle-shaped piece of glass or plastic, called a **prism**.

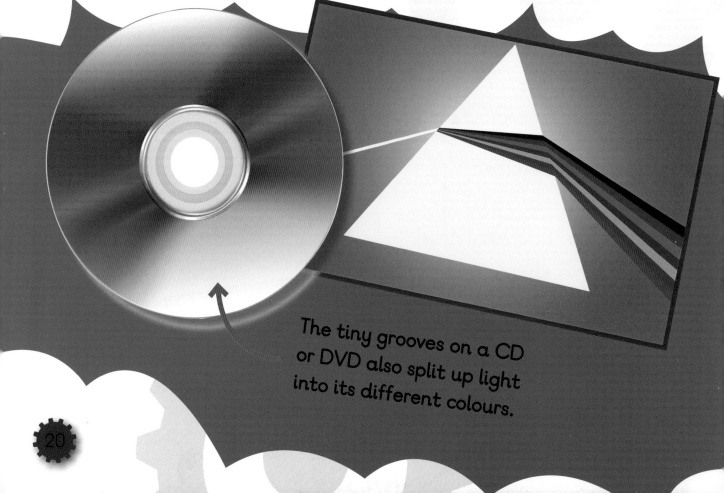

The tiny grooves on a CD or DVD also split up light into its different colours.

20

You will need: a torch, a piece of white paper and a prism.

1 Shine the torch through the prism.

2 Hold the paper on the other side of the prism. Can you see all the colours?

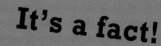

It's a fact!

As the light passes into and out of the prism, it bends, or refracts. This splits the light into many colours.

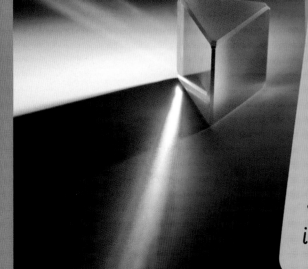

A rainbow forms when raindrops act like tiny prisms. They split up white sunlight into all its colours.

21

GLOSSARY

Daylight
Light from the Sun that shines on us during the day.

Electricity
A kind of energy that can be used to make machines work.

Light source
Something that gives out light, such as a torch or lamp.

Opaque
A material that does not allow light to pass through. Opaque materials are not see-through. They are the opposite of transparent.

Prism
A triangular piece of glass or clear plastic. When light shines in and out of a prism, it bends and splits into separate colours.

Pupil
The hole in your eye that lets in light.

Reflect
To bounce off a surface and change direction. Light reflects off mirrors and other objects.

Refraction
The way light bends when it passes from one see-through substance into another.

Shadow
An area of darkness that is made when an opaque object blocks the path of light.

INDEX

NEXT STEPS

※ For all activities involving sunlight, remind children never to look directly at the Sun, as it can damage eyesight.

※ Look out for shadows in everyday situations. Discuss the conditions that create sharp shadows, such as bright sunlight or a strong, single light source. If there are a lot of lights in a room, or if the Sun is behind clouds and its light is spread out across the sky, shadows become blurred or unclear. Discuss with the children why this might be.

※ See how many light sources the children can see at any one time, including the Sun, electric lights, candlelight and small LED lights on phones, watches and computers. They could make a list of all the light sources they can find and describe whether the light is white or coloured, and whether they think it is bright or dim.

※ Planets and the Moon seem to shine in the night sky, but they are not light sources. Encourage children to work out why they seem to shine. Planets and the Moon reflect light from the Sun, making it bounce back to us on Earth. This happens even when we can't see the Sun. So moonlight is actually light from the Sun, reflecting back at us.

※ Encourage the children to look in a mirror. Ask, 'Why can you see yourself?' Light from a light source bounces off you, and hits the mirror. It reflects back off the mirror and into your eyes.

※ For another refraction experiment, dip a straw into a glass of water. Move it this way and that and look at it from different angles. It will sometimes appear bent because refraction bends the light travelling from it.